Dear Parents/Caregivers:

Children learn to read in stages, and all children develop reading skills at different ages. **Fisher-Price® Ready Reader Storybooks**™ were created to encourage children's interest in reading and to increase their reading skills. The stories in this series were written to specific grade levels to serve the needs of children from preschool through third grade. Of course, every child is different, so we hope that you will allow your child to explore the stories at his or her own pace.

Book 1 and Book 2: Most Appropriate For Preschoolers

Book 3 and Book 4: Most Appropriate For Kindergartners

Book 5 and Book 6: Most Appropriate For First Graders

Book 7 and Book 8: Most Appropriate For Second Graders

Book 9 and Book 10: Most Appropriate For Third Graders

All of the stories in this series are fun, easy-to-follow tales that have engaging full-color artwork. Children can move from Books 1 and 2, which have the simplest vocabulary and concepts, to each progressive level to expand their reading skills. With the **Fisher-Price® Ready Reader Storybooks**™, reading will become an exciting adventure for your child. Soon your child will not only be ready to read, but will be eager to do so.

Educational Consultants: Mary McLean-Hely, M.A. in Education: Design and Evaluation of Educational Programs, Stanford University; Wendy Gelsanliter, M.S. in Early Childhood Education, Bank Street College of Education; Nancy A. Dearborn, B.S. in Education, University of Wisconsin-Whitewater

Fisher-Price® Ready Reader Storybook™

Sherman Came for a Visit

Book 5

Written by Susan Kochan • Illustrated by Dudley Moseley

Modern Publishing
A Division of Unisystems, Inc.
New York, New York 10022

Here is my aunt May.
Here is Sherman, her dog.

When they came to visit,
Mom wished he was a frog.

My brother tried to ride him.

Sherman hated that.

My sister tried to dress him.

He ate her hat.

Dad tried to take a nap.

Sherman woke him up.

I tried to drink my juice.

Sherman took my cup.

When he heard his favorite
person at the door,

Sherman raced across
the floor.

When he found Grandma,
our family's other guest,

she said, "Hello, Sherman!
You are the best."

Grandma rubbed his belly.
She scratched behind his ears.

When we ate lunch, Grandma said, "He is so dear."

Sherman was a good dog for the rest of the day.

But we knew what he would do when Grandma went away.